YOUR COFFEE, PIZZA AND WINE

Your Coffee, Pizza and Wine

VINCENT JAMES

Coffee, Pizza and Wine

Copyright © 2021, 2022 by Vincent James

All rights reserved. No part of this book may be reproduced in any manner whatsoever without written permission except in the case of brief quotations embodied in critical articles and reviews.

First Printing, 2021
Second Printing, 2022

1

Coffee

YOUR MOODS

you are always hope,
no matter what mood you're in,
you make us better

YOUR LIKABILITY

I may not like all
that you love, but I will still
love all that you like

YOUR FIRST COFFEE WITH ME

and this single cup,
feels like it will last all day—
hope you stay with me

YOUR PREVIOUS RELATIONSHIP

don't look for him in
the past you thought you shared, but
he never lived through

YOUR PERFECTLY-TIMED INNER VOICE

when the time is right,
no one else will know to tell
you "hey, time to go"

YOUR
JUST-GETTING-BY-MOMENTS

the just getting by
moments we share are— our great
opportunities

YOUR NIGHT AND THEN YOUR DAY

imagine your dreams
as billions of stars— shining,
to guide wakefulness

YOUR DAILY OPINIONS

taking time to share
your every word— here with me,
is gratifying

YOUR FIRST IMPRESSION

I knew right away
you would impact my life in
some life-changing way

YOUR GREATEST LAZY MORNING

build a pillow fort,
for our protection from all
errands this morning

YOUR REQUEST TO TAKE IT SLOW

my love will slow down
when needed to match, step by
step, your gentle pace

YOUR EVERYDAY HOLIDAY

combining visions—
make our boring rituals
feel like holidays

YOUR SECOND IMPRESSION

I know you're unlike
anyone I've met, but you
must respect my space

YOUR BAD-DAY NARRATIVE SO FAR

knowing what you want,
but not living that way— as
motivation waits

YOUR EX

just because
you want
to be in her life,
it doesn't give
you the right to take
away from her happiness
by being in it

YOUR UNDERNEATH-BLANKET JOKES

blanket canopy—
underneath which you whisper
your funniest jokes

YOUR HONEYMOON PHASE

I can't think straight when
you're on my mind, so I take
a moment with you

YOUR INTUITIVENESS

I waited years to
find you, but sensed who you were
long before we met

YOUR NEVER-ENDING NIGHTS

to nights we don't want
to end, may they stay with us
each night we're apart

YOUR FIRST MORNING HUG

our sleepy embrace—
my motivation up to
the end of the day

YOUR PROPOSAL

days were all the same
til your love kneeled to propose
a different life

YOUR OTHER SUNLIGHT

the rain falls angry
on you, but can't extinguish
the light inside you

YOUR VIEW THROUGH THE CEILING

so don't be afraid—
you were meant to rise above
your ceiling of doubt

YOUR ADULTING BREATHING EXERCISE

take a deep breath in,
pausing to stop the impulse—
then breathe it all out

YOUR PREFERRED APPETIZERS

all the worldly tastes—
among all the plates chosen
with love, between us

YOUR OLD GHOSTS

ghosting someone may
be ghosting a part of you
that you're afraid of

YOUR LAUGHTER-GRIN

your best grin happens
when you're kind of embarrassed
from laughing so hard

YOUR FAVORITE COFFEE SHOP AGAIN

sensing your smile
behind me while I stand in
line for our coffees

YOUR WARMED-OVER COLD MORNING

feelings of winter
warmed over by added scents
of roast coffee beans

YOUR UNDREAMED DREAMS

there is something vast
in everything you'll be, but
not yet imagined

YOUR NON-SMILING DAYS

and so everyday,
we'll find your smile, even
on non-smiling days

YOUR INTERESTS

your interests now
interest me since you are
always interesting

YOUR HIGHER CLIMB

you thought you made it,
but the mountain gets higher—
we take a deep breath

YOUR DANCE

rhythm in your hips—
power to move continents—
shakes down to my core

YOUR EXPERIENCE-ONLY WISDOM

let's keep it simple,
for complications to know,
they need resolving

YOUR WARM AURA ON A COLD DAY

holding our coffees
in the cold, then warmed by your
glow as you approach

YOUR WAYS OF TESTING ME

rather than complain,
I will honor how you test
me to earn your trust

YOUR NEXT CHAPTER

every place you've been
that hurt you— now elevates
you through darker paths

YOUR OXYGEN

our deepening love,
laying awake, filling up—
the room— with breathing

YOUR BALANCE WITH BOUNDARIES

a lack of balance
with setting boundaries invites
negativity

YOUR WORDS YOU DON'T SAY

power in silence—
the words you don't say— mean more,
strengthened by stillness

YOUR LOVE THROUGH EVERYTHING

accept the struggles,
and love deepens and deepens
till challenge is joy

YOUR KEEPER

you know they're worth it
when you can sense they miss you,
when you miss them too

YOUR
TEXTING-BETWEEN-THE-LINES

responses between
their text messages slows down,
to give you space too

YOUR CONVERSATIONAL SKILLS

conversations with
you always leave me speechless,
when you speak my mind

YOUR GOOD BOREDOM

inner discipline
creates good boredom and laughs
at dull distractions

YOUR SOURCES

tender honesty
reveals untapped sources for
calming dialogue

YOUR STEP BACK FROM IT ALL

seek restraint and calm,
and love will find you gently—
fear evacuates

YOUR QUALITY SLEEPING TIME

so when you're sleeping,
I try so hard to sleep too—
for more time with you

YOUR WAKING-ME-UP ABILITIES

you awaken my
life from a purgatory
of boring routine

YOUR HERE AND NOW

wishing you had been
in my life before, but you
deserve my best now

YOUR COFFEE-SHARING

sleepy wasteful thoughts
and worries won't last morning,
since you made coffee

YOUR VIBE FROM BEING NEXT TO YOU

in the dark with you,
I'm filled with a greater glow,
than the brightest sun

YOUR COMBINED SCENT

our meeting of scents—
your perfume with my cologne—
the smell of date night

2

Pizza

YOUR PARTY SMILE

celebrate moments
in each day like holidays
with a party smile

YOUR HELP

I helped you so much,
but learned it wasn't how you
wanted to be helped

YOUR INFLUENCE

you made me want to
live my best life for me, but
I didn't know you

YOUR EXPRESSIONS

I love every smile,
hope, opinion, memory,
dream and laugh you have

YOUR LOVE LESSONS

some relationships
won't end well, but you will learn
love from everything

YOUR YEARS BEFORE US

the empty years of
not knowing you prepared me
to learn all of you

YOUR LOVE WILL STILL FILL YOU

always choose love— you
may not be loved in return—
love can still fill you

YOUR QUIRKS

beauty in patterns—
all your familiar habits—
refreshing to me

YOUR
JUST-BEING-YOU-STRENGTH

your armor and shield
creates a broader sword
for your protection

YOUR JOURNEY
UP-TO-THIS-POINT

the culmination
of events that brought you here
needs your gratitude

YOUR GENTLE MELLOW PRETZEL

gentle mellow vibes—
our closeness felt in crossed legs
pretzeled on the couch

YOUR STILLNESS FIREFLIES

arriving stillness
settles around us like lit
fireflies sequenced

YOUR GRADUATION

you wish for more time,
but you fill time with a life
you don't want to live

YOUR COLLABORATION

life is telling us
that we can do more than this—
only together

YOUR OWN UNIQUE PACE

I learn to enjoy
the 'waiting for you process'—
worth it every time

YOUR DIFFERENT VERSIONS OF YOUR BEST

you bring out the best
in us with each version of
how we're meant to be

YOUR TURN BUT I'VE GOT THIS

taking turns on chores,
we serve each other from deep
love that transcends roles

YOUR PATIENCE FOR BOTH OF US

you show me patience
I never had for myself
when we need it most

YOUR RED-FACE

to me, you're a queen,
even when your face is red,
and you've been crying

YOUR EVOLVING UNIQUENESS

all the unique things,
only you can offer each day—
find your openness

YOUR VERY IMPORTANT LITTLE EXTRAS

the little extras
you never feel like doing
that make others smile

YOUR WEATHER REPORT

the weather changes,
love changes, yet we're cold when
we won't change with them

YOUR EIGHT-BIT PIZZA PLACE NOSTALGIA

cozy arcade lights—
soft eight-bit sounds drone and hum—
a quaint cabinet

YOUR DEEPER DEEP

you hold a power—
found deeper than consciousness—
beneath all the doubt

YOUR BEST MOMENTS

feel it for moments—
escapable good feelings
that someday might last

YOUR LIFETIMES

I would spend lifetimes
just to show you there is more
to you than you know

YOUR NEW FAVORITE IMPERFECTIONS

naked in summer—
vulnerability crossed
with new confidence

YOUR VALUES EMERGING

raging inner love
crying out as suffering—
deepening your joy

YOUR WINTER-EVENING WALK

white string lights in trees
warm us like our scarves, along
winter avenues

YOUR SOLAR SYSTEM

change tilts my orbit
but my world revolves around
you and no one else

YOUR BECAUSE

because of you, love
fills me with compassion for
others needing love

YOUR BEST LOVE

you taking care of
yourself means more to me than
how far we will go

YOUR RELATIONSHIP-PACE

learn not to try too
hard when love needs you
to exert patience

YOUR ALMOST-NAP-TIME MOMENT

the almost nap-time
euphoria— together
we lay, holding hands

YOUR STARTING-OVER GOALS

in starting over,
seeds may be planted deeper
than patience permits

YOUR BEACH

foaming waves, bare feet,
and our laughter between sounds
of splashing ocean

YOUR STAY-AT-HOME DECISION

gentle steamy tea,
the softest blanket— restful,
contemplative, mood

YOUR CIRCLING ADVENTURE

we always come back
to us, wherever we are,
on this sweetest ride

YOUR CULTURE

learning your culture
taught me to love you in ways
never known to me

YOUR RENEWABLE WEDDING VOWS

not just pictures, gifts,
dances, vows, but looking in
your eyes— when we pause

YOUR PREGNANT-CRAVE

creativity
in the way your ordering
pregnant-crave pizza

YOUR STRONG POINTS OF VIEW

rolling fields in waves
show eternity's picture
of your boundless strength

YOUR TRUSTED VOICE

when my unique pain
may not permit any in,
you greet them for us

YOUR PERSONAL FEEDBACK

choices you make on
your worst days will tell you how
much progress you've made

YOUR MOTIVATIONAL SKILLS

once I fell for you
my life felt complete as though
all my goals were reached

YOUR DESERVING INTUITION

thoughts of you daily—
to send the positive vibes
you always deserve

YOUR RESTAURANT EXPERTISE

the other couple
keeps staring at our pizza—
we'll share our knowledge

YOUR UNRECOGNIZED SPONTANEOUSNESS

finding together
over pizza in the bed
makes it all better

YOUR FRIENDS YOU'VE OUTGROWN

your life without them
can reveal life within you
they concealed from you

YOUR NECESSARY MINDFUL NAP

problems everywhere
that won't subside today—
we've earned a short nap

YOUR LATE NIGHT AFTER-AN-ARGUMENT

staying up real late—
night of epic disclosure—
our new beginning

YOUR DAILY LOVE MEDITATION

love more powerful
than daily grind distractions
that keeps you present

YOUR COMMITMENT

commitment guides you
even when motivation
has left you behind

YOUR EXTRAORDINARY ORDINARY

our ordinary
lives feel extraordinary
when we're together

3

Wine

YOUR FAVORITE WINE AND DRESS

the great tasting wine
spills all over your dress, but
you smile from the wine

YOUR PRESENCE IN THE SAME ROOM

whenever you're near,
I smile a little bit more
just knowing you're here

YOUR EXPERIENCES

there's no way to learn
but with experience this
time and you've got this

YOUR GREATEST ACHIEVEMENTS

even your greatest
victories often start out
as losing battles

YOUR BREAKING THE GENERATIONAL CYCLE

life beyond childhood—
undoing what our parents did
by teaching our kids

YOUR SILENT TREATMENT

days without talking
to you last like empty years
filled with hushed regret

YOUR SUNSET BLANKET

the sunset blankets
your day's stress in pink and blue—
an orange glow too

YOUR LIFE DESERVES YOUR LOVE

love your life before
you'll meet more people who try
to tell you not to

YOUR IMMEDIATE AND LONG-LASTING REFLECTION

our kids mirror us,
so we mirror each other—
family reflections

YOUR CRICKET MUSIC

shared Thursday wine glass
by a stone fire pit with
only the crickets

YOUR POINT OF ORDER

your observations
form a mirror that shows me
how the world sees me

YOUR LOVE REQUIREMENTS

love may require
letting go of everything
to deepen our love

YOUR PRESENCE IS A PRESENT

your extra time here
challenges my demons to
relinquish my soul

YOUR
NOW-ACKNOWLEDGED-OLD-BURDENS

inadvertently,
pain unforgiven transmits
to everyone else

YOUR SELFLESSNESS

learning to give, when
you feel like you have nothing
to give, fills your heart

YOUR MUCH-DESERVED-BREAK

we will make a mess—
then deny, argue and breathe,
in grateful stillness

YOUR IMPACT AS A DAUGHTER, SISTER, WIFE AND MOTHER

life's much more than this—
you're doing more than you know—
just by existing

YOUR AWESOME FAMILY TREE

water each other
through dialogue, shared pain, moments—
we grow as one tree

YOUR QUIET-WINE-TIME

thinking about all
the same things with you over
silent sips of wine

YOUR HANDS ARE COLD

we'll let the cozy
fireplace do the talking,
as we hold both hands

YOUR HOLIDAY MOOD

holiday coldness
by extended family
thawed by your kind soul

YOUR NEXT LEVEL

you deserve better
than how you beat yourself down
when life provokes you

YOUR LINGERING ESSENCE

somehow you're sitting
with me when I'm alone now—
your essence calms me

YOUR LEGACY

your unique version
of beautiful will never
be replicated

YOUR HOPE WE LATER SHARE

hope stares us both down
after a three-way fight— till
we apologize

YOUR TIMELESS

days go by faster
and we're older, but with you,
time always stands still

YOUR VICTORY-LAP

climb out of doubt, then
crawl back in, as many times
as needed, to win

YOUR BAD RELATIONSHIPS

punishing yourself
with bad relationships will
stall self-forgiveness

YOUR DEFINITION OF PERFECTION

"good enough" partners
with "doing your best" to be
your brand of "perfect"

YOUR NEW PEOPLE

notice you attract
others who reflect how you
feel about yourself

YOUR
DEEPER-THAN-LOVE-FEELING

that warmest feeling—
the one only you and I
ever know and share

YOUR STRESSED-OUT

we will exercise
together to help you break
through your stressed-out slump

YOUR 2AM COZY

familiar breathing
and rolling over patterns
make our sleep cozy

YOUR PHOTOSYNTHESIS

like an ancient oak—
wind-bloomed and storm-awakened—
our love thrives with age

YOUR ONLY

there is no one else,
and gratitude grows each day
that there's only you

YOUR REWRITTEN CHAPTERS

you get more chances
in this life, but you still have
to show you've earned it

YOUR RENEWED MISTAKES

your mistakes stay with
you until you're ready to
learn something from them

YOUR GOOD

you've renewed the good
in me when I'd forgotten
good was ever there

YOUR EVERYDAY OPPORTUNITIES

each day you can find
new opportunities to
learn the depth of love

YOUR LOVE-SMILE

though I won't love all
that you love, I'll love your smile
through all that you love

YOUR BED-TIME LANGUAGE

your body language
calming the entire room as
you make our kids laugh

YOUR GIFT OF HINDSIGHT

learning our lessons,
then tying them back to love
in a tighter bow

YOUR LATEST MODEL

every new version
of you is one I fall in
love with every time

YOUR PARTYING LIKE WHEN WE WERE YOUNGER

time passes quickly
at parties when you're older—
embrace these moments

YOUR LOVE WILL COME FULL CIRCLE

I will wait as long
as you need for you to love
you as you love me

YOUR WAY HOME

your deepest fears stay
until you've introduced them
to your ambitions

YOUR REVOLUTION

spiritual pain
reopens wounds, for healing
opportunities

YOUR CIRCUMSTANCES CHANGE

doubts become your realm
of possibilities when
they're all you'll look for

YOUR HIDDEN BURNOUT

know to let go when
flames around you burn brightest
to bring back your glow

YOUR
HISTORY-STILL-BEING-WRITTEN

shared memories change
as they evolve and deepen
with our connection

YOUR INVALUABLE CONTRIBUTIONS

you help me win all
my battles against myself
just by being here

YOUR ENCOURAGEMENT

I always needed
to be liked until you showed
me how to be loved

YOUR LOVE MATTERS MOST

when love matters most,
distractions and excuses
have nowhere to hide

YOUR OPTIONS

I choose you each day,
before, during and after
our days together

www.ingramcontent.com/pod-product-compliance
Lightning Source LLC
Chambersburg PA
CBHW070043120526
44589CB00035B/2277